Tides of Time -
Poems on Living and Loving

Deepika Unni

BookLeaf
Publishing

India | USA | UK

Tides of Time - Poems on Living and Loving
© 2024 Deepika Unni

All rights reserved.

No part of this publication may be reproduced, stored in a retrieval system, or transmitted, in any form or by any means, electronic, mechanical, photocopying, recording or otherwise, without the prior written permission of the presenters.

Deepika Unni asserts the moral right to be identified as the author of this work.

Presentation by *BookLeaf Publishing*

Web: www.bookleafpub.com

E-mail: info@bookleafpub.com

ISBN: 9789360942687

First edition 2024

Dedicated to my daughter Rhea,
who is the greatest joy of my life

ACKNOWLEDGEMENT

To all the people who have crossed paths with mine on this journey of life, I extend my heartfelt gratitude. Each one of you has left an indelible mark on my being, shaping me in ways beyond measure. Whether through lessons taught, shared journeys, the warmth of love, or the stark absence thereof, you have contributed to the person I am today.

It is with deep appreciation that I dedicate my first book of poems, "Tides of Time", to each one of you. Your presence in my life has fueled my creative spirit and made this publication possible. Thank you for being a part of this beautiful voyage.

Whispers of a Poet's Heart

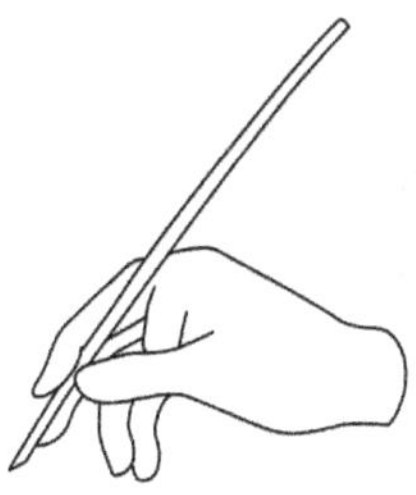

*T*he pen flies,

Pages turn,
A world unfurls,
A book of poems—
A poet's pearls.

But doubts arise,
A nagging fear,
Will anyone read?
Come anywhere near?

Yet in each verse
A whispered plea,
To touch a heart,
To set thoughts free.

But what should I write about,
I wondered?

Write of love,
Of life's journey,
Compose odes to the sun,
To a lover's sigh,
Or delve into darkness,
Just let emotions fly.

For in this book
A glimpse of my soul,
A kaleidoscope of tales
A part of my whole.

So, let it be penned,
Each line with care,
In hopes that someone, somewhere,
Will actually open its cover,
Take a look inside
And find something for themselves,
Some hope
A warm embrace.

My Baby girl

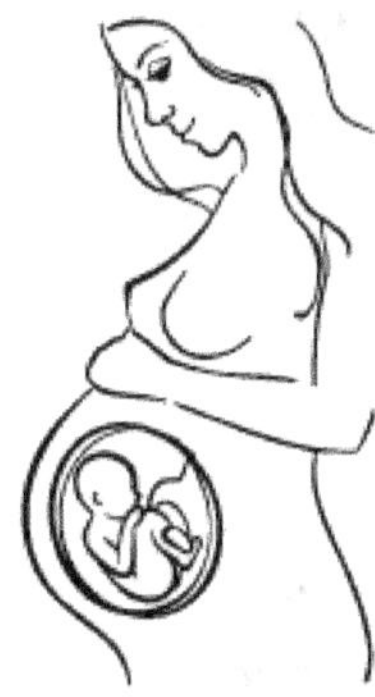

Ever since you have gone away
My days are so empty.
Pain
Guilt
Loneliness
Sorrow
Are all constant companions.

I prayed for you
I cherished you,
I kept you safe and secure inside me,
I nurtured you
I dreamt of you,
I wanted you to be with me soon.

Together K & I,
We started dreaming of a family,
Of a perfect little baby
Who would bring us such joy
A perfect family we would be.
We didn't care
If you were a girl or a boy.

Unfortunately,
God had other plans
Which we couldn't ever imagine.
He called you back to him so soon.
And left us with nothing.

Sometimes
When I look up at the night sky
And see the stars shining bright,
I know that you are
The brightest little star up there,
Looking over me,
Keeping me safe.

God, keep my baby with you
And send her back to me.
Because you see,
I love her so much
And I want her back with me.

Happy Birthday Sweetheart

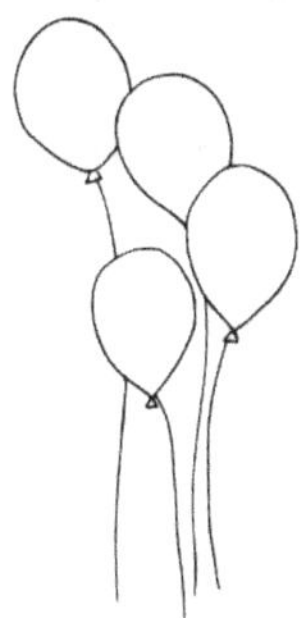

Happy Birthday Sweetheart
My sweet sweet child!

One month ago
You were born to us.
A daughter we had prayed for,
A child we would've cherished
And loved to pieces forever more.

On this special day of yours,
Our one wish for you
Is one of peace.
We pray to God
To keep you safe
And send you back to us.

Till then sweetheart,
Know that we love you,
And that we will always remember you.

Whatever happens to us in our lives,
You will be
Our first and most loved daughter,
Forever!

Where am I headed?

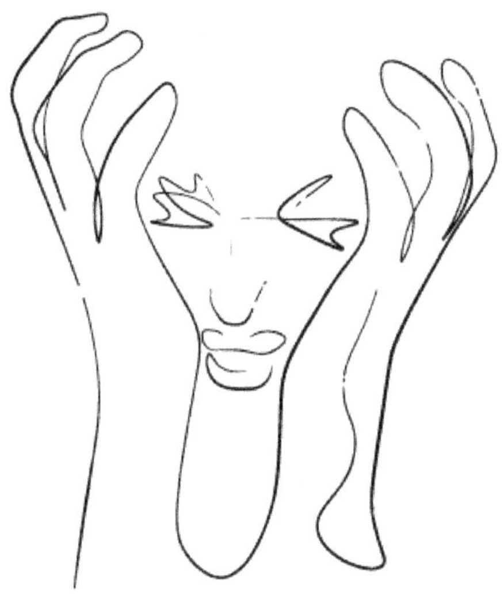

What I had set out to be
And what I've become!
What I had imagined
And what I have done.!
God knows what will happen,
The road is rough.
Decisions are never easy,
And life is too f*"#&-ing tough !!

Fernweh & Wanderlust

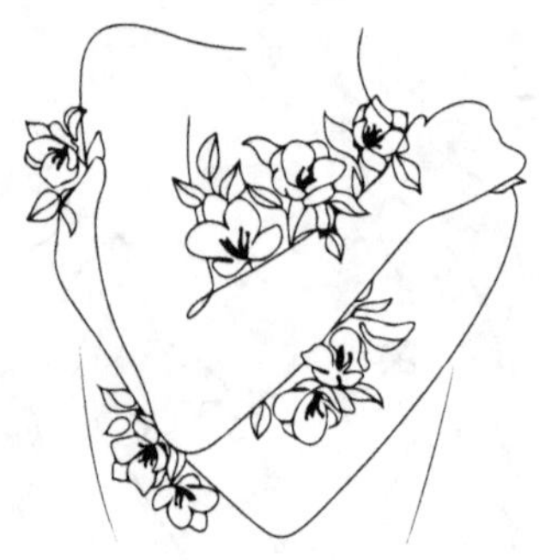

Fernweh
Wanderlust
Every opportunity I get,
Travel I Must.

Bulbuls, long winding roads,
Silver oaks and sprouting weeds.
The unresponsive sky
Had evoked in me
A response
Unexpected and uncanny.

Where staying put was overrated
And for which I couldn't care two hoots,
Now,
I want to trade wings for roots.

Coonoor: A Love Story for me

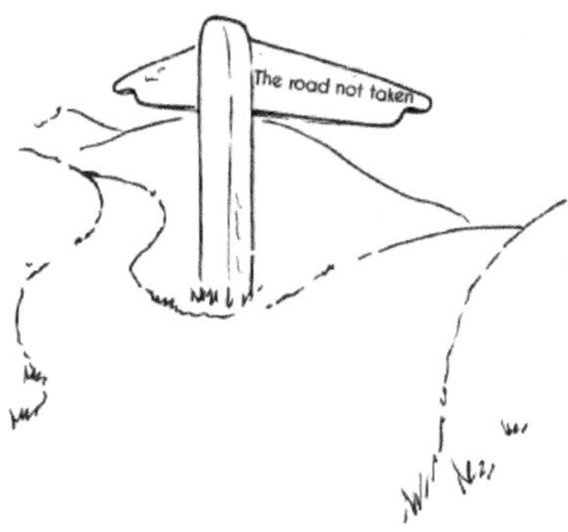

In the heart of change
Where the whispers flow,
A small town beckons
A tale to bestow.

Grown weary of the city's relentless race,
I found solace anew in a quaint embrace.
Nestled beneath skies that painted dreams,
A canvas of simplicity, or so it seems?

Streets lined with stories
Of a bygone day,
Where old timers linger
Remembering days spent in play.

The air
A symphony of nature's song.
I felt in my bones
I truly belong.

In the arms of a town
So warm and small,
I discovered love anew
And embraced its call.

The old town haunts
Where memories reside,
With Bisons, Bears and Leopards
Leaving us wide-eyed.

Each building
A witness to history's dance,
Generations ago
When someone came to take a chance.

The 100-year-old bakery
Brimming with local delight,
The scent of the best filter kaapi
Next to the dentist,
A paradoxical invite!

In the midst of tea gardens,
And there where for a brief moment

Two cars stood still,
I surrendered my heart
Against my will.

For this small town
Where I feel at home,
Has robbed me of my wanderlust
And my desire to roam.

Young old folk
With tales in their eyes,
Keepers of secrets
Under starlit skies.

The kindness of neighbours
A gentle balm,
In this small town
An incredible calm.

Falling in love
Not jut with the town,
But with the people
All with ups and downs.

A mosaic of moments
Woven in glee,
Coonoor: a love story for me.

Nilgiris in the Rains

*M*ist and rain
Wrap Arunachala in a blanket.
I can hardly see
Beyond the first line of trees,
The giant monstera leaves
Dripping wet
Shedding rain drops
As if being squeezed.

The yellow Datura
Visible yet obscure,
The grass below
Squishy and lush green.
The flowering bushes,
Trembling and unsure
Of the Sun's appearance

As nothing above is seen.
The distant trees
Are just shadows.
Apparitions
One reads in Gothic novels.

All's quiet,
No birds sing, no cat meows,
Waiting for the howl
Of the hound of Baskervilles.

But wait!
Who's that in the garden walking?
Umbrella on shoulder,
Not minding the weather?
One hand holding
Some food for a seedling
The other, dropping it like dew from a feather.

It must be the gardener
The redoubtable Mani,
Unmindful of the rain
The mist, and the weather,
Come to look after his plants
Which are mainly
Waiting for his touch and care
That's tender.

Nilgiris in the rains
Transforms into a show,
Presenting vistas
Changing every moment
As in the Japanese classical dance Butoh
From within, not without
Comes each movement.

The mist swirls,
The rain falls gracefully,
The nearest trees
Also recede from view.

My eyes and my heart
Revel in this beauty.
I wouldn't trade it
For a King's treasury.

Borrowing from Christopher Marlowe
Here would I dwell
For Heaven's in these dales
And all is dross and callow.
Outside Arunachala and the Nilgiri vales.

A March Afternoon in Coonoor

In Coonoor's embrace,

A March afternoon's delight,
Where sun-kissed hills
Meet the azure sky so bright.

Amidst the chaos of plains
Where heat holds sway,
A cool breeze whispers secrets,
In a gentle ballet.

Oh, the joy it brings,
This refreshing air,
As if nature herself, for a moment,
Does care.

Through emerald tea gardens,
It softly glides,
Whispering tales of respite,
Where peace abides.

Unabashed & Uncompromising

Why do I need to change?

Why must I change my nature?
Just because society doesn't like it?
Or because "men will misunderstand?"

If the problem is in understanding,
Then should the ignorant not be educated?
Or should the book be altered
To suit the ignorant?

I struggled with this 20 years ago
When I returned from Dubai
As a single woman and mother,
Suddenly being "attractive" to men
Because they saw availability and opportunity.

Once again, I find myself in a new place,
Having to decide how to be.
Should I be myself?
And let the misunderstandings happen,
And deal with them as they come?
Or should I "be less open with the men"
And sit around parties and not engage?
Or engage only with other women?

This is not who I am.

Energy, strong, open, open mind
Full body hugs and no gender differentiation,
Dance with the women and the men,
Walk with the women and the men.
That is me.

And I like me.

Then why do I need to be punished?
And asked to be a different me?
Why must I listen to society?
And fit in a box, neatly labelled?
Why is it ok to be me
Only if I have a man by my side
As my protector?

Some women are allowed to be themselves
Because they have a ring on their finger.
Just because I took off the ring,
I am not afforded the same luxury.

Do I want to succumb?
Because I want to live in this small town?
Or do I live on my own terms?
Unabashed, uncompromising!

Sunrise at Tiger Hills

In the Nilgiris,
Where whispers weave through
Misty veils of dawn,
Where the sun's first hue
Creeps like a shy secret upon the hills,
Awakening life in silent thrills.

A palette of pastels
Paints the sky,
Soft strokes of pink and gold,
As birds fly
In graceful arcs,
Their songs a gentle hum,
Nature's orchestra—
The day's first strum.

The mist, a tender veil,
Begins to lift,
Revealing secrets,
A whispered gift,
Of valleys deep and forests green,
In this tranquil dawn
A world unseen.

Freedom

While dancing,
I shed all masks,
Free from confines,
In the energy, I bask.

Uninhibited,
My spirit flies,
Through rhythmic beats,
My heart complies.

For in the dance,
I am whole and true,
Expressing myself
In all that I do.

It's where my heart
Finds its song,
And where
I truly do belong.

His eyes

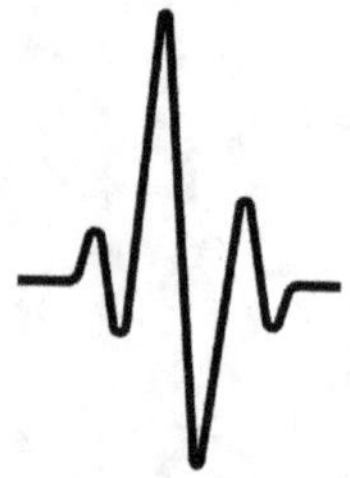

In the depths
Of the shola's deep embrace,
Eyes of tiger,
A glowing grace.

Amidst the shadows,
A piercing spark,
Watching silently
From the dark.

Ten long minutes,
No sound disturbs
The forest's hush,
Just the tiger's eyes,
A burning rush.

Then with silent stealth,
They fade
Into the night
A secret made.

Leaving me
With wonder stark,
Of the tiger's eyes
In the shola dark.

The Magnificent Nilgiri Langur

Amidst the whispering leaves,

In the ancient embrace of Nilgiris,
I found
A sentinel of time,
A Titan
Cloaked in fur and shadow.

Perched aloft
The verdant throne,
Majestic, aloof,
Yet somehow near.

A creature
Of ebony and silver grace,
Unfurled its form
In tranquil, arboreal space.

Each movement
A testament,
To the rhythm
Of untamed wilderness.

In his eyes ,
The wisdom of ages,
Etched in the lines
Of weathered bark.

And as I stood below
A humble guest,
Captivated
By this elusive grace,
I glimpsed a glimpse
Of something primal,
A connection
To the heart of untamed spaces.

A vision,
A sigh,
A fleeting sight,
In the realm of treetops,
A sacred space
Where the Nilgiri langur
Reigns in sovereign grace,
A testament
To nature's enduring embrace.

His deep voice going "*who who who*"
Echoing through the trees,
Adding to the symphony
Of nature's mysteries.

I Miss You

*In the quiet corners
Of my days,
Thoughts of you
Drift like a haze,
Across the miles
A world apart,
Missing you—
Tugs at my heart.*

*Vancouver's lights,
So bright and bold,
Yet they can't warm
This empty fold
Where your laughter
Used to play.
Now distant,
I miss it each day.*

Memories dance
A bittersweet waltz,
Of bedtime stories
And childhood tears.

How swiftly time
Has slipped away,
Leaving me
With echoes of yesterday.

In every sunset's
Golden hue,
I send my love
Sincere and true.

Hoping it finds you
Where you stand,
In Vancouver's embrace
So very grand.

Though the miles
May stretch and strain,
Know my love for you
Will always remain.

An unbroken thread
A steady line,
Binding our hearts - Yours and mine.

My Joy, My Pride

In robes of accomplishment
You stand tall,
My daughter, my pride,
Answering life's call.

Through years of dedication
You have strived!
Now, a graduate
Your dreams revived.

Each step,
A testament to your sheer might,
Through sleepless nights
And morning's light.

From the first day
Uncertain yet bold,
To this moment,
Stories forever told.

You've conquered mountains
Overcome strife,
And now stand
At the threshold of a new life.

As you walk
Across that stage with grace,
A smile
Adorning your glowing face,
I stand in awe
Of your journey so far,
Proud of you -My beautiful star.

Your degree
A testament, a treasure untold,
A future of possibilities
Brightly unfold.

In this moment
My heart takes flight,
For Rhea
My baby, my utmost delight.

My chosen Solitude

Alone
Yet not lonely,
I navigate
This space.

My own
Where silence resonates.
In solitude's embrace
I find my voice.
Crafting a life
By my own choice.

No footsteps echo
Save for mine alone,
No opinions sway
But those I've sown.

Responsibility,
A weight I bear,
Yet freedom's song
Whispers in the air.

A canvas blank
Awaiting my design,
In this self-made world
I redefine.

Living on my own
A journey profound,
In solitude's embrace,
My true self is found.

The Trellis of the Rosewood bed

There's no scale in the world

That can measure his love for her.
But he can express it,
In a slight touch,
In a single kiss.

In just a single word,

ACUSHLA

He can express the entirety of his love.

Where does he go
Bearing all that love
When his time comes and he sheds
This mortal coil?

This love will tie him down
To that trellis on the rosewood bed.
From where he'll keep gazing at her
Full of love and longing,
Even after his breath has become air.

The room at the top of the stairs

My heart skipped a beat,
When in the crowd, I found him.
There he was,
Looking dapper in his suit.

That voice, that smile,
Brings a rush of desire,
For time spent
In the room at the top of the stairs.

You see beneath the mask I wear

In the quiet spaces
Where we connect,
A bond beyond romance,
Yet deeply set.

You, my last man standing,
In a warm embrace,
Grasping all my quirks
With gentle grace.

Through fears and dreams
You walk by my side,
Understanding depths
Where emotions reside.

Beneath the Darth Vader mask
I wear for the world's eye,
You see the truth and accept ATDs
Never asking me why.

With laughter as our song
And jests our flight,
You're the wind beneath my wings
Shining bright.

In your company
I find solace and ease,
Deepest love
Dancing on life's breeze.

The Starlit Stage

In the twilight of fifty-three years lived,
A stage awaits,
With its tales to give.

Nervous energy,
A fluttering beat,
Heart dances wild
In this grand feat.

Fear,
A companion, by my side,
When the curtains open,
There will be no place to hide.

The script,
A map of uncharted lands,
Lines to remember
Like shifting sands.

The moment nears,
A trembling hand,
Stepping forth
Into the unknown land.

Words unfurl,
A symphony in the air,
Characters breathe
Alive and fair.

Through the scenes
A waltz of delight,
Fear subsides,
Replaced by the light.

Embracing the role
With every breath,
Heart pounding madly
Within my chest.

Do I hear laughter?
Do I hear applause?
For the courage found
In these ageing claws?

For the first time
On this stage so grand,
I found myself
Learning to expand.

The Joys of Menopause

Really? The Joys of Menopause?

Let's not pretend—
A rollercoaster ride,
With no clear end.

Hot flashes
Hit like a summer sun's wrath,
My hormones are putting me
On a crazy warpath.

One minute I'm freezing,
Next, I'm a sauna,
My thermostat is broken,
Don't accuse me of being a Prima Donna!

Sleep?
Oh, what a hilarious joke,
Tossing and turning,
It's no gentle poke.

My memory's
Playing hide and seek,
Words vanish mid-sentence,
So to speak.

"I had it just now,
It was right here!"
I am dancing on the stings
Of an unknown Puppeteer.

And don't get me started
On mood swings galore,
I'm a weepy mess,
Then a lion's roar.

They said it's a phase,
It'll all pass by,
But right now,
All I want to do is cry.

So here's to the women,
In menopause's grip,
Laughing and crying,
Doing a flip.

We'll survive this journey,
Tough as nails,
With humour intact,
Even when sanity fails!

A piece of me still lives in Bombay

In the heart of Bombay
Where dreams are spun,
Streets alive with flavours,
Under the blazing sun.

A love affair
With each spicy bite,
A symphony of tastes,
Oh what a delight!

From vada pav's embrace,
A love so true,
To savouring pav bhaji and ganne ka juice,
Feeling renewed.

Yet it's not just the food
That steals my heart,
But the rhythm of life,
A mesmerising art.

The hustle, the bustle,
The city's beat,
In every step,
A new tale to greet.

The trains that weave
Through the city's veins,
A lifeline of stories,
Joys, and pains.

Movies, theatre, plays,
Concerts galore,
In your embrace,
Each moment I have adored.

Now far away,
My heart does occasionally ache,
For the love of Bombay,
No distance can break.

Riot of Colours

In Coonoor's gardens,
A riot unfurls,
A canvas of colours,
A whirl of swirls.

Daisies dance with joy,
Their petals bright,
Amidst Agapanthus,
A celestial sight.

Roses whisper
Tales of love's sweet embrace,
Hibiscus blushes
With elegance and grace.

Bougainvilleas cascade
In vibrant hue,
Irises stand tall
In the morning dew.

Melastomas weave
Their purple spell,
Bleeding heart creepers
With stories to tell.

Bear's breeches reach out
With gentle touch,
Fuchsias bloom,
A painter's clutch.

Each flower a verse,
A poem untold,
In this symphony of colours
Magical and Bold.

Where beauty reigns
Soothing every heart,
In every Coonoorian's garden
A masterpiece of art.

The Magic of Podcasting

In the realm
Where voices dance and sing,
I found my joy,
A podcast's wing.

A channel
Carved from dreams untold,
Where tales and thoughts
Find a foothold.

With mic in hand,
I embark each week,
To weave narratives
In a unique way, I seek.

Some conversations deep,
Connections bloom,
A shared journey
Through joy and gloom.

Listeners tune in
From far and wide,
A community
Where voices collide.

So here I stand,
With grateful heart,
For podcasting,
A wondrous art.

Discovering, hosting,
I'll forever be
In love with this world,
Where creativity flows free.

My Feline Love

They lounge on books with ancient lore,
Curled up in blankets, they explore.
In quirky ways, they claim their throne,
A regal presence, all their own.

From playful pounces to quiet purrs,
Their world, a stage, so rich, so pure.
With every leap, a boundless grace,
In their enigma, a sacred space.

For in their beauty, wit, and flair,
Cats weave a spell beyond compare.
A blend of grace and mystery,
They reign in quiet sovereignty.

Kindness

In a world that rushes,

Always in a hurry,
Kindness often overlooked,
In such a flurry.

To be gentle, to be kind,
A quiet art,
Yet seldom noticed
In the fast-paced part.

A nice person, a gentle soul,
So rare,
Their value unseen
In the daily glare.

In a realm of noise,
Of hustle and bustle,
Being soft-hearted
Can seem like a tussle.

Though not prized
In today's fast-paced race,
A nice person shines
With a quiet grace.

For in a world
That often forgets to see,
Their kindness whispers,
"This is the way to be."

A Java lover in Tea country

In a land of tea,

Oh what a sight,
She dared to sip her coffee,
Bold and bright.
Amongst the leaves of green
And tea plantation rows,
She raised her cup
Much to everyone's "ohs"!

The locals stared,
Wide-eyed surprise,
As she took her filter decoction
To their tea-filled skies.
"Isn't that like bringing coal to Newcastle?"
They jested,
But for her caffeine fix,
She bravely protested!

With each sip, she chuckled,
Feeling quite the rebel,
In this sea of tea,
She stood out like a pebble.
But oh, the aroma,
The flavour so grand,
As she enjoyed her coffee
In this tea-loving land!

So here's to the odd,
The quirky, the funny,
Drinking coffee 'mongst fields
Where tea's sunny.
For in this mismatch,
There's joy to be found,
A java lover in tea country,
Quite renowned!

The Jacaranda Avenues

Just the other day
We drove a little far away
And opened our eyes for the first time, it
seemed
And discovered a lavender dream.

Canopy's of Jacarandas
And carpets of them too
Across the vales and hillside
Gaze in wonder, is all we could do.

Tales of beauty,
Their blossoms weaved,
All across the Nilgiris,
You had to see it to believe.

Be it Selas, Kotagiri, Ooty or Coonoor,
The countryside coloured anew.
Purple, Lilac and Lavender drew
Everyone to the Jacaranda Avenues

www.ingramcontent.com/pod-product-compliance
Lightning Source LLC
Chambersburg PA
CBHW061715130726
47996CB00006B/2327